Cambridge Little Steps 1

Numeracy Book

Lorena Peimbert

Cambridge Little Steps 1

Number 1

Present
Number 1

👁 Look. 2¹₃ Count. ✏ Color.

Number 1

Presentation: Children open their books. Point to the picture of the school. Say: *This is a school. School.* Children repeat: *School.* Ask: *How many schools can you see? Let's count! One. One school.* Children count along with you. Write a large number 1 on the board. Then point to it and say: *One.* Children repeat. Finally, children color the number 1 and the school.

Practice: Play music. Children stand up and dance. Stop the music and show children one crayon. Ask: *How many crayons can you see? Let's count! One.* Children say *one* as they hold up one finger. Then play the music again, pausing to show children a school object, such as a book, a table, or a chair, and have them count it: *One.*

3

👁 Look. ✏ Color.

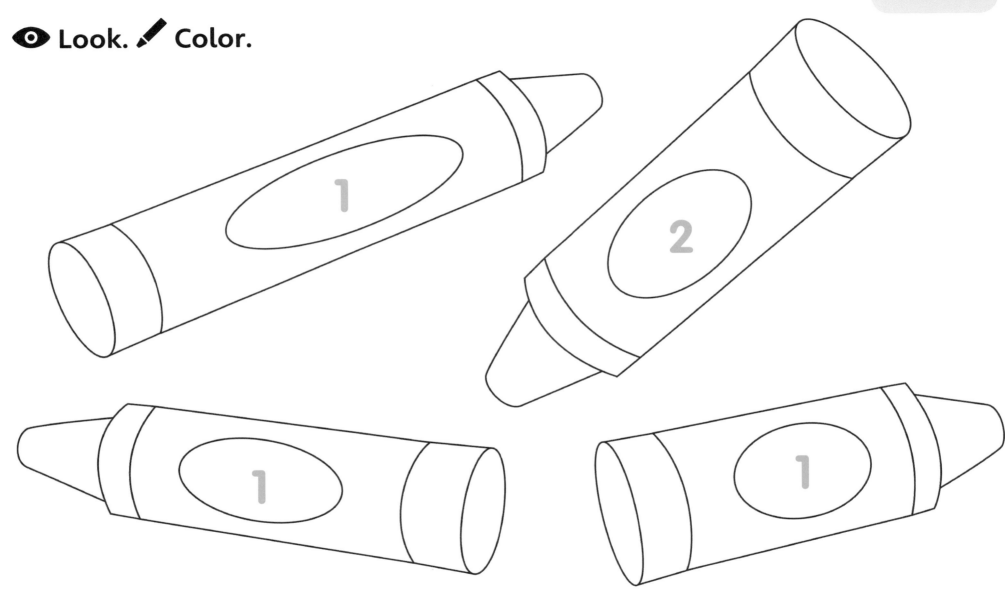

Presentation: Make cards with the numbers 1 and 2. Show children a card with the number 1. Children identify the number: *One.* Then show a card with the number 2. Ask: *Is it number one? (No.)* Repeat with the remaining cards. Finally, children open their books and look for and color only the crayons with the number 1 on them.

Practice: Display the number 1 and 2 cards on the board so the numbers aren't visible. Individual children go to the board and turn over a card. Ask: *Is it number one?* If it is, the child says *yes* and claps once. If it isn't, the child says *no* and sits down. Repeat this procedure until all cards have been turned over.

👁 Look. 2¹₃ Count. ⬭ Trace.

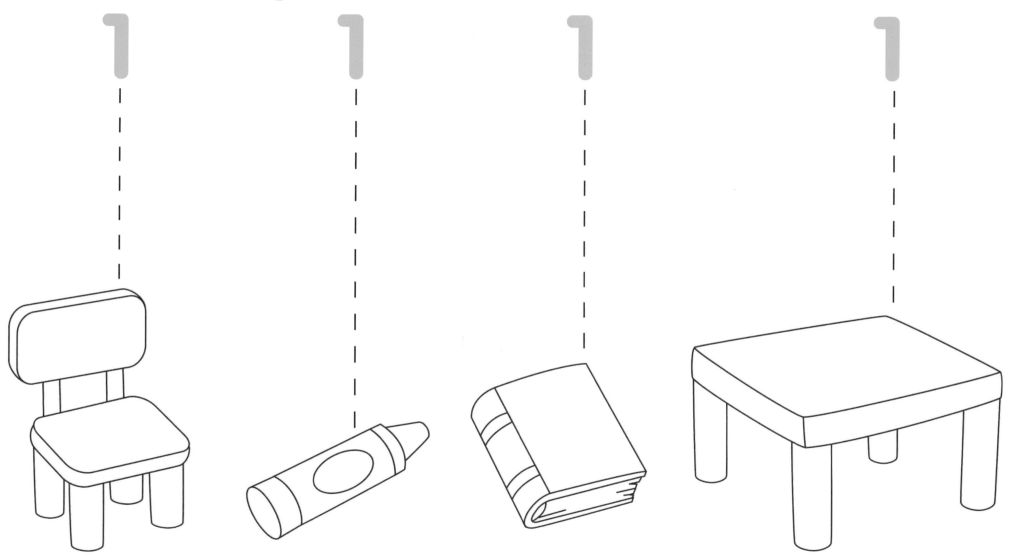

Presentation: Make cards with the number 1 in different fonts and various cards with drawings of one school object. Show children the number 1 cards and display them on the board. Children say *one* and jump once. Then show the school object cards. Children name the items. Display the object cards under the number 1 cards and say *One [chair]* as you draw a line from each number 1 to each object. Children repeat. Finally, they open their books. They look at each number 1 and count the corresponding object. Then they use a crayon to trace the line.
Practice: Put the number 1 cards in one bag and the school object cards in another bag. Children sit in a circle. Play music and have children pass the two bags around together. Stop the music. The child with the bags pulls out a card from each bag, looks at them, and says: *One [chair]*. Repeat until all children have had a chance to participate.

👁 Look. 2⅓ Count. ⭕ Trace.

Presentation: Draw a large number 1 on the board. Point to it and say: *One*. Children repeat. Trace a number 1 in the air as you say *one*. Children do the same. Then point to yourself and say: *One teacher*. Children repeat after you. Show other school objects (one of each). Children count and name the objects. Finally, they open their books, count the teacher, and trace the numbers.

Practice: Give each child a sheet of construction paper with a big number 1 on the left side. Children use finger paint to paint the number 1 with their fingers. Then they paint or draw one school object of their choice. Children can take their artwork home.

2 Number 2

👁 Look. 2¹₃ Count. ✏ Color.

Presentation: Have a boy and a girl go to the front of the classroom. Point to the boy. Ask: *Is he a boy or a girl? (Boy.)* Repeat with *girl*. Then ask: *How many children can you see? Let's count! One, two. Two children.* Children count along with you. Write a large number 2 on the board. Point to it and have individual children repeat after you: *Two.* Finally, they open their books, count the children, and color the number 2.

Practice: Children stand up. Play music and have children walk around the classroom. Say: *Make groups of two!* Children hold hands in pairs. Then they count as they point to themselves and their partner: *One, two!*

👁 Look. ✏ Color.

Presentation: Make cards with the numbers 1 and 2 on them. Show children a card with the number 2. Children identify the number: *Two.* Then show a card with the number 1.
Ask: *Is it number 2? (No.)* Repeat until you've gone through all of the cards. Finally, children open their books and look for and color only the parts of the picture that have a number 2 on them.

Practice: Display the number 1 and 2 cards around the classroom. Play a tambourine or other percussion instrument as children walk to the rhythm (fast or slow). Stop playing and say:
Go to number 2! Children go quickly to a number 2 card and touch it.

👁 Look. 2⅓ Count. 📖 Match.

2 -

2 -

2 -

Presentation: Invite two girls or two boys to the front. Give each child a book. Ask: *How many [girls] can you see? Let's count! One, two. Two [girls]*. Write the number 2 on the board. Point to it and say: *Two*. Children repeat. Finally, they open their books. They count and trace the lines to match each number 2 to the corresponding pair of children.

Practice: Put cards with the number 2 on the board. Place cards with the following pictures around the classroom: one boy, two boys, one girl, two girls, one crayon, two crayons, one table, two tables, one book, and two books. Invite a child to find a card: *Find two boys*. The child finds the correct card, counts the boys in the picture, and puts the card below a number 2. Repeat until all cards with two objects have been found.

👁 Look. 2¹₃ Count. ◯ Trace.

Presentation: Draw a large number 2 on the board. Point to it and say: *Two*. Children repeat. Trace a number 2 in the air as you say *two*. Children do the same. Then display two objects. Point to the objects and ask: *How many can you see?* Children count and say *two* as they hold up two fingers. Finally, they open their books, count the children, and trace the numbers.

Practice: Give each child a sheet of construction paper with a large number 2 on the left side. Distribute balls of crumpled-up tissue paper in a variety of colors. Children glue the paper balls onto the number. Then they draw two body parts of their choice on the right side. Children can take their artwork home.

Number 3

👁 Look. 2¹₃ Count. ✏ Color.

Presentation: Invite three children to the front of the classroom. Ask the class: *How many children can you see? Let's count! One, two, three. Three children.* Say: *Dance!* The three children dance. Then say: *Stop!* Invite another group of three children to the front of the classroom. Repeat the procedure, asking children to do different actions, such as jump, run (in place), or kick. Write a large number 3 on the board. Point to it and have individual children repeat after you: *Three.* Finally, they open their books, count the children, and color the number 3.

Practice: Children stand in a circle. Play music and have children move together to the right or to the left. Then stop the music and say: *Clap your hands three times!* Children clap with you. Repeat by asking children to do a different action three times. Model each action.

11

👁 Look. ✏ Color.

Presentation: Make various cards, each with the number 1, 2, or 3 on it. Show children a number 3 card and have them identify the number: *Three.* Then show a card with a number 1 or a number 2. Ask: *Is it number 3? (No.)* Repeat until you've gone through all of the cards. Finally, children open their books and look for and color only the chairs with the number 3 on them.

Practice: Play *Musical Chairs.* Attach cards with the numbers 1, 2, and 3 to the chairs. Play music. Childen dance around to the rhythm. Then stop the music. Children can sit only in the chairs with the number 3.

👁 Look. 2⅓ Count. 📖 Match.

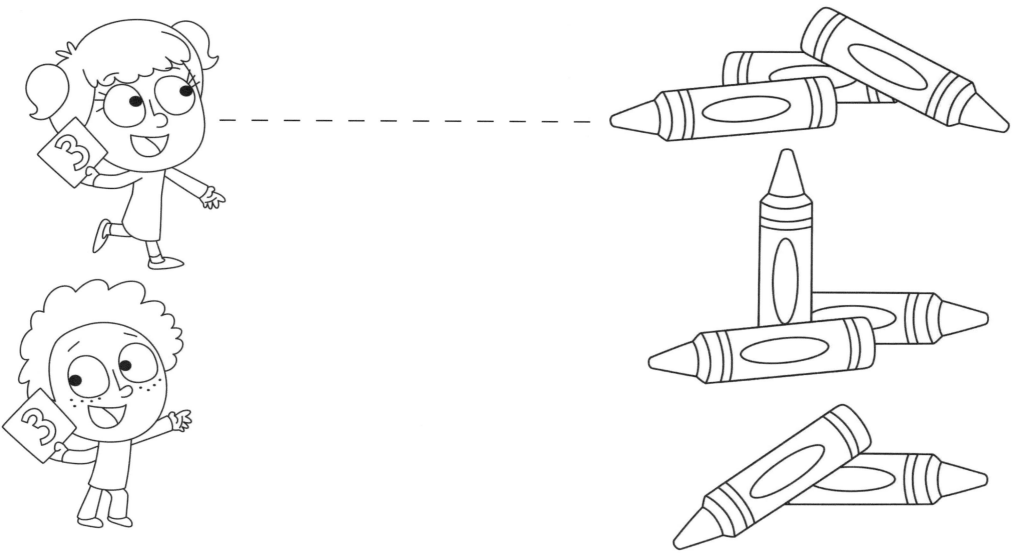

Presentation: Make cards with the number 3 and cards with one, two, or three items that children can identify. Hold up a card with three items. Children count the items and say *three*. Display the remaining object cards on the board and place the number 3 cards around the classroom. Invite a child to find a number 3 card and attach it below a card with three objects. Finally, children open their books. They count and trace or draw lines to match the children to the groups of three crayons.

Practice: Play a game of *Memory* on the board with the number 3 cards and the object cards. If one card has a number 3 and the other has three objects, it's a match, and the child takes the cards and sits down. If it's not a match, the child turns the cards back over and sits down. Repeat until children match all cards.

👁 Look. 2¹₃ Count. ⭕ Trace.

Presentation: Draw a large number 3 on the board. Point to it and say: *Three*. Children repeat. Trace a number 3 in the air as you say *three*. Children do the same. Then display three objects. Point to the objects and ask: *How many can you see?* Children count and say *three* as they hold up three fingers. Finally, they open their books, count the children, and trace the numbers.

Practice: Give each child a sheet of construction paper with a large number 3 on the left side. Distribute pieces of pasta. Children glue the pasta onto the number. Then they draw three children doing different actions. Children can take their artwork home.

4 Number 4

👁 Look. 2¹₃ Count. ✏️ Color.

Presentation: *Make cards with one family member on each card (mom, dad, sister, brother, baby, grandfather, grandmother). Display a group of four family members. Point to the family members and elicit the words. Ask: How many family members can you see? Let's count! One, two, three, four. Four family members. Children count along with you. Repeat with other card combinations. Then write a large number 4 on the board. Point to it and have individual children repeat after you: Four. Finally, children open their books, count the family members, and color the number 4.*
Practice: *Have children stand up. Play music. Then stop the music and have children clap, jump, or stomp their feet four times as they count. Repeat as many times as you wish.*

👁 Look. ✏ Color.

Presentation: Make cards with the numbers 1, 2, 3, and 4. Show children a card with the number 4. Children identify the number: *Four.* Then show a card with the number 1, 2, or 3. Ask: *Is it number four? (No.)* Repeat until you've gone through all of the cards. Finally, children open their books and look for the number 4 in the picture. They color only the baby.

Practice: Display the number cards around the classroom. Say: *Walk to number four!* Children walk to a number 4 card and stop. Repeat by asking children to run (slowly), crawl, dance, or jump to a number 4 card.

👁 Look. 2$\frac{1}{3}$ Count. 📓 Match.

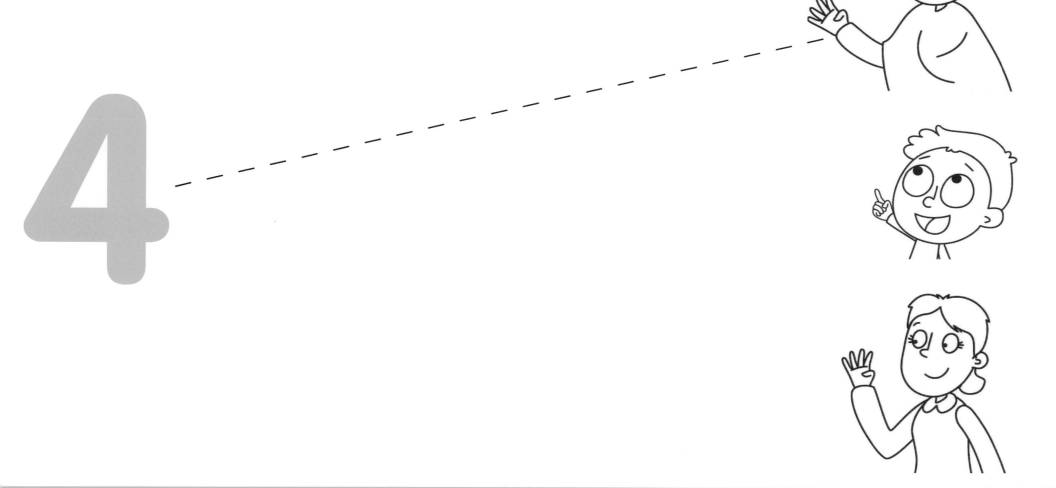

Presentation: Put various cards with the numbers 1, 2, 3, and 4 in a bag. Play music. Children pass around the bag. Then stop the music. The child with the bag pulls out a card, says the number, shows the correct number of fingers, and counts. Finally, children open their books. They count and trace or draw lines to match the number 4 to the family members holding up four fingers.

Practice: Have children sit in small groups. Distribute the number cards along with any other small objects you have available. Children look at the number and count the corresponding number of objects. Then they place the objects on top of the card.

17

👁 Look. 2¹₃ Count. ⬭ Trace.

Presentation: Draw a large number 4 on the board. Point to it and say: *Four.* Children repeat. Trace a number 4 in the air as you say *four.* Children do the same. Then display four objects. Point to the objects and ask: *How many can you see?* Children count and say *four* as they hold up four fingers. Finally, children open their books, count the family members, and trace the numbers.

Practice: Give each child a sheet of construction paper with a large number 4 on the left side. Distribute small sticks or other natural objects and have children glue them onto the number. Then they draw four family members of their choice to the right of the number. Children can take their artwork home.

5 Number 5

👁 Look. 2¹₃ Count. ✏ Color.

Presentation: Make cards, each with five drawings of a pet from the unit. Hold up a card and have children say the name of the pet. Then ask: *How many [cats] can you see? Let's count! One, two, three, four, five. Five [cats].* Children count along with you. Repeat with the remaining cards. Finally, children open their books. They count and color the hamsters, then they color the number 5.

Practice: Divide the class into teams of five. Give all five members of each team a headband with a picture of the same pet on it. Children stand in a circle. Play music. Children dance to the rhythm. Then stop the music and say: *Fish in the circle!* Children with the fish headbands go to the center of the circle and act like fish. Count the fish with children.

👁 Look. ✏️ Color.

Presentation: Make various cards with the numbers 1, 2, 3, 4, and 5. Show children a card with the number 5. Children identify the number: *Five.* Then show a card with the number 1, 2, 3, or 4. Ask: *Is it number five? (No.)* Repeat until you've gone through all of the cards. Finally, children open their books and look for and color the dog with the number 5 on it.

Practice: Display the number cards on the board. Then attach a card with a dog, cat, bird, rabbit, or fish below each number. Children sit in a circle. Play music as children pass around a ball. Stop the music. The child with the ball says the name of the pet under number 5 and pretends to be it. Change the animal under number 5 and repeat.

👁 **Look.** 2¹₃ **Count.** 📖 **Match.**

Presentation: Make a memory game with various cards with the numbers 1 to 5 and cards with one to five items, such as pets, family members, or school objects. Put the cards face down along the board. A child goes to the board and turns over two cards. Then the child says the number and counts the items. If they match, the child takes that pair. Repeat until all of the cards have been matched. Finally, children open their books. They count and trace or draw lines to match the number 5 to the books with five items.

Practice: Draw a large number 5 on the board. Point to it. Children say *five*. Give each child a blank card. Children draw five pets, family members, or school objects of their choice. Play music and pass around a ball. Stop the music. The child with the ball holds up his or her card, counts the drawings, and attaches the card to the board next to the number 5.

21

👁 Look. 2$\frac{1}{3}$ Count. ⬭ Trace.

Presentation: Draw a large number 5 on the board. Point to it and say: *Five.* Children repeat. Trace a number 5 in the air as you say *five.* Children do the same. Then display five objects. Point to the objects and ask: *How many can you see?* Children count and say *five* as they hold up five fingers. Finally, children open their books, count the birds, and trace the numbers.

Practice: Give each child a sheet of construction paper with a large number 5 on the left side. Distribute small pieces of colorful paper and have children glue them onto the number. Then they draw five pets of their choice to the right of the number. Children can take their artwork home.

6 Number 6

👁 Look. $2\frac{1}{3}$ Count. ✏ Color.

👁 Look. ✏ Color.

Presentation: Make various cards with the numbers 1, 2, 3, 4, 5, and 6. Show children a card with the number 6. Children identify the number: *Six.* Then show a card with a different number. Ask: *Is it number six? (No.)* Repeat until you've gone through all of the cards. Finally, children open their books and look for and color only the items with the number 6.

Practice: Children sit in a circle. Show the number cards one by one. Children say the numbers. When you show number 6, children count to six, stand up, and switch seats. Repeat the game as many times as you wish.

👁 Look. 2¹₃ Count. 📖 Match.

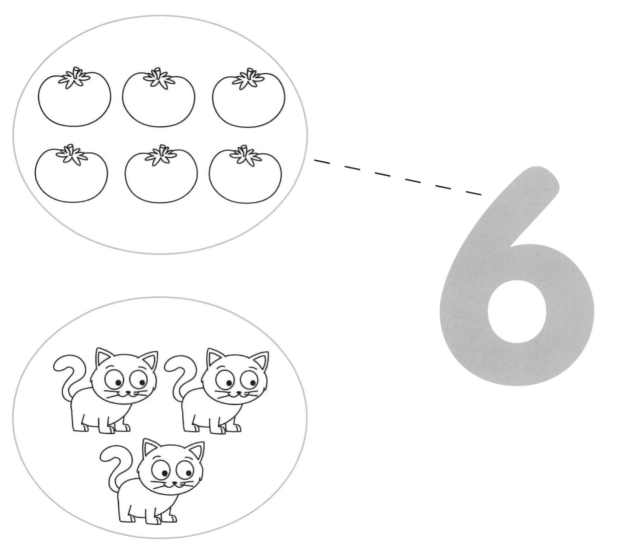

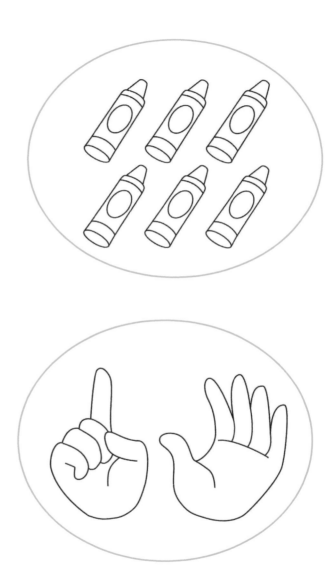

👁 Look. 2¹₃ Count. ⬭ Trace.

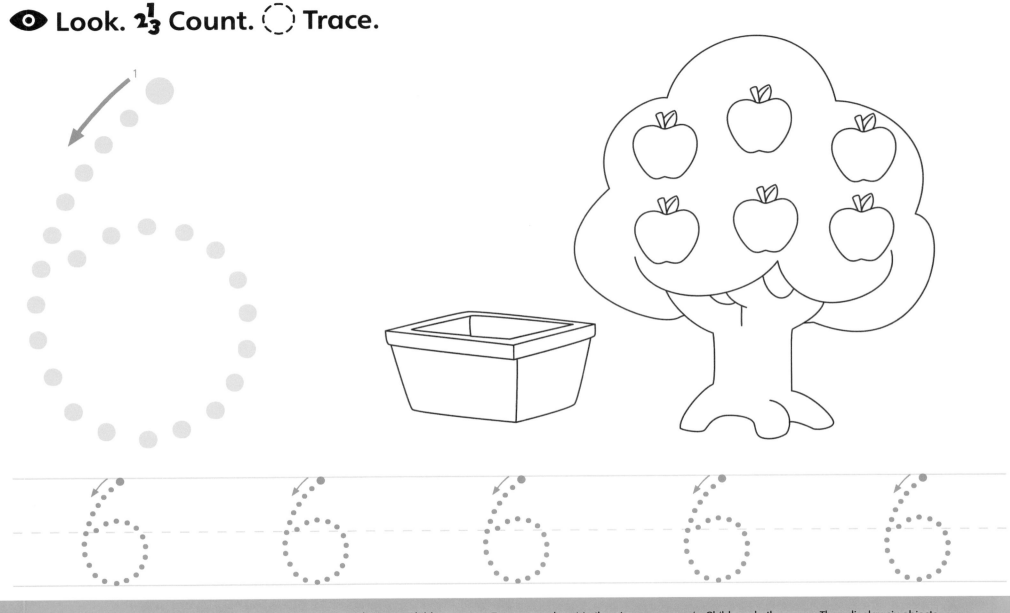

Presentation: Draw a large number 6 on the board. Point to it and say *six*. Children repeat. Trace a number 6 in the air as you say *six*. Children do the same. Then display six objects. Point to the objects and ask: *How many can you see?* Children count and say *six* as they hold up six fingers. Finally, children open their books, count the apples, and trace the numbers.

Practice: Give each child a sheet of construction paper with a large number 6 on the left side. Distribute small circles cut from different-colored paper and have children glue them onto the number. Then they draw six fruits or vegetables of their choice. Children can take their artwork home.

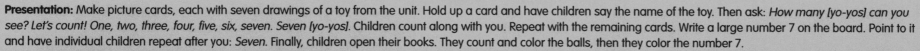

7 | Number 7

👁 Look. 2¹₃ Count. ✏ Color.

Presentation: Make picture cards, each with seven drawings of a toy from the unit. Hold up a card and have children say the name of the toy. Then ask: *How many [yo-yos] can you see? Let's count! One, two, three, four, five, six, seven. Seven [yo-yos].* Children count along with you. Repeat with the remaining cards. Write a large number 7 on the board. Point to it and have individual children repeat after you: *Seven.* Finally, children open their books. They count and color the balls, then they color the number 7.

Practice: Display the picture cards on the board at a height children can reach. Call a child to the front and say: *Point to the [dolls] and count them.* Write the number 7 below the card and have the child trace the number. Repeat with other students and the remaining cards.

27

👁 Look. ✏ Color.

Presentation: Make various cards with the numbers 1, 2, 3, 4, 5, 6, and 7. Show children a card with the number 7. Children identify the number: *Seven.* Then show a card with a different number. Ask: *Is it number seven? (No.)* Repeat until you've gone through all of the cards. Finally, children open their books and look for and color only the boxes with the number 7.

Practice: Display seven boxes. Put a toy inside a few of the boxes. Attach a number 7 card to the boxes with a toy and other number cards to the other boxes. Count from one to seven as children pass a ball. When you say *seven*, the child with the ball finds a box labeled with a number 7, opens it up, and names the toy inside. Repeat with the remaining boxes.

👁 Look. 2¹₃ Count. 📖 Match.

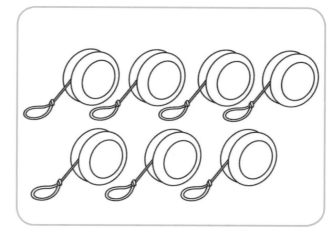

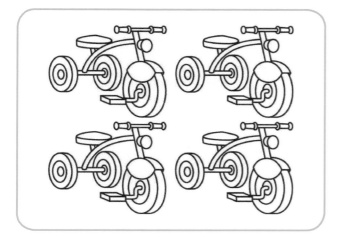

Presentation: Make various picture cards with one to seven toys, fruits, vegetables, pets, family members, or school objects. Show them to children one at a time. Children name and count the items. If the card has seven items, children stomp their feet seven times. Repeat with the remaining cards. Finally, children open their books. They count the items in the squares, then they trace or draw lines to match the number 7 to those squares.

Practice: Display the picture cards on the board. One child goes to the back of the classroom. Give the child a piece of paper. Say: *Hide seven [yo-yos]!* The child walks quickly to the board and hides the corresponding card with the paper. Repeat as many times as you wish.

👁 Look. 2¹₃ Count. ◯ Trace.

Presentation: Draw a large number 7 on the board. Point to it. Children say *seven*. Trace a number 7 in the air as you say *seven*. Children do the same. Then display seven objects. Point to the objects and ask: *How many can you see?* Children count and say *seven* as they hold up seven fingers. Finally, they open their books, count the children with kites, and trace the numbers.

Practice: Give each child a sheet of construction paper with a large number 7 on the left side. Distribute small square pieces of paper in various colors and have children glue them onto the number. Then they draw seven toys of their choice to the right of the number. Children can take their artwork home.

Number 8

👁 Look. 2¹₃ Count. ✏ Color.

Presentation: Make picture cards, each with eight drawings of something children can see in the park (flowers, trees, bees, butterflies, clouds, swings, slides, seesaws, monkey bars). Hold up a card and have children say the name of the object. Then ask: *How many [butterflies] can you see? Let's count! One, two, three, four, five, six, seven, eight. Eight [butterflies].* Children count along with you. Repeat with the remaining cards. Finally, children open their books, count and color the flowers, and color the number 8.

Practice: Write a large number 8 on the board. Display the picture cards around the classroom. Then toss a ball to a child. That child says *one* and tosses the ball to another child, who says *two*. Continue until children reach *eight*. The child who says *eight* stands up, looks for the card you call out, counts the objects, and displays the card next to the number 8.

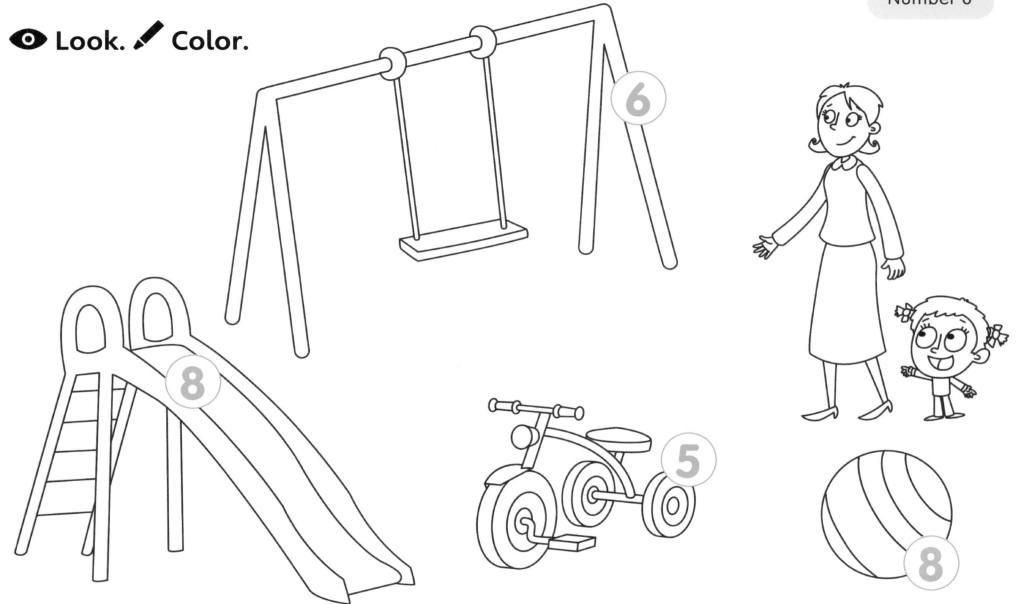

👁 **Look.** ✏ **Color.**

Presentation: Make various cards with the numbers 1, 2, 3, 4, 5, 6, 7, and 8. Show children a card with the number 8. Children identify the number: *Eight.* Then show a card with a different number. Ask: *Is it number eight? (No.)* Repeat until you've gone through all of the cards. Finally, children open their books and look for and color only the objects with the number 8 in them.

Practice: Display on the board the picture cards from the previous activity with groups of eight things you can see at the park. Then place the number cards below them face down and at a height children can reach. A child goes to the front and turns over a number card. If it's a number 8 card, ask: *What can you see at the park?* The child answers according to the picture card above it: *I can see [butterflies].* If it's not a number 8 card, the child turns the card over and sits down. Repeat as many times as you wish.

2$\frac{1}{3}$ Count. ▉ Match.

Presentation: Make cards with groups of one to eight things we can see at the park. Show them to children one at a time. Children name and count the items. Finally, children open their books and count the items. Then they draw lines to match the number 8 to the triangles containing eight items..

Practice: Make a memory game with various cards that show things we can see at the park and the corresponding number cards. Display the cards facing down on the board at a height children can reach. A child turns over two cards. If the number of items on the picture card and the number match, the child takes the pair. If a child turns over a card with eight items and a card with the number 8, everybody claps eight times. Repeat until all the cards have been matched.

👁 Look. 2¹₃ Count. ⭕ Trace.

Presentation: Draw a large number 8 on the board. Point to it. Children say *eight*. Trace a number 8 in the air as you say *eight*. Children do the same. Then display eight objects. Point to the objects and ask: *How many can you see?* Children count and say *eight* as they hold up eight fingers. Finally, they open their books, count the children, and trace the numbers.

Practice: Give each child a sheet of construction paper with a large number 8 on the left side. Distribute small dried flowers and other objects from nature and have children glue them onto the number. Then they draw eight things that can be found in the park on the right side of the sheet. Children can take their artwork home.

Numbers 9 & 10

(9)

👁 Look. 2⅓ Count. ✏ Color.

Presentation: Make cards, each with nine or ten drawings of things children can see near where they live: houses, farms, buildings (with 9 or 10 windows), toy stores, markets, parks. Hold up a card with nine items and have children say the name of the object or place. Then ask: *How many [houses] can you see? Let's count!* Children count along with you. Repeat with the remaining cards. Then repeat this procedure to introduce the number 10. Finally, children open their books. They count and color the windows, then they color numbers 9 and 10.

Practice: Write a large number 9 and a large number 10 on the board. Put the cards with nine and ten pictures in a bag and play music. Children pass around the bag until you stop the music. The child holding the bag when the music stops pulls out a card and counts the drawings on it. Then the child places the card below the corresponding number on the board. Repeat as many times as you wish.

■ Match. ✏ Draw. ✏ Color.

Presentation: Make various cards with the numbers 1, 2, 3, 4, 5, 6, 7, 8, 9, and 10. Show children a card with the number 9. Children identify the number: *Nine.* Then show a card with a different number. Ask: *Is it number nine?* (*No.*) Repeat until you've gone through all of the cards. Do the same to introduce number 10. Finally, children open their books, look at the speech bubble of each child, and say the number. Then they match the number with the number on the child's house, draw a line to the house, and color the house.

Practice: Display the number cards around the classroom. Ask for two volunteers. Say: *Jump to number nine!* Count to nine. The first one to get to a number 9 wins. Alternate the actions children have to do to get to the numbers. They can also run, walk, fly, swim, crawl, or do other actions. Repeat to review number 10.

👁 Look. 2¹/₃ Count. ✏ Color.

9

10

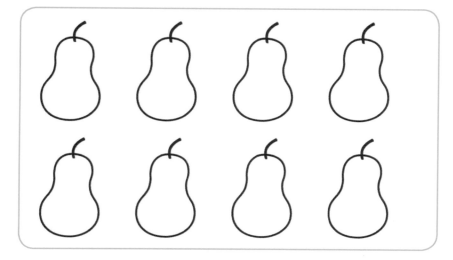

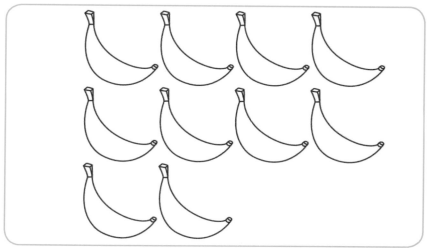

👁 Look. 2¹₃ Count. ⬭ Trace.

Presentation: Draw a large number 9 on the board. Point to it. Children say *nine*. Trace number 9 in the air as you say *nine*. Children do the same. Then display nine objects. Point to the objects and ask: *How many can you see?* Children count and say *nine* as they hold up nine fingers. Repeat this procedure with the number 10. Finally, children open their books, count the doors and the windows, and trace the numbers.

Practice: Give each child a sheet of construction paper with a large number 9 on the left side and a large number 10 on the right side. Distribute a variety of materials for children to glue onto the numbers. Children can take their artwork home.

1	2	3	4	5
6	7	8	9	10

Children cut out the cards and play *Concentration* in pairs. First, they set the cards on the table. Then they alternate turning the cards over. Children get to keep the cards where the dots and the number match. The child with the most number of cards wins the game.